PREHISTORIC LIFE

VERTEBRATES

BY CLARE HIBBERT AND RUDOLF FARKAS

Gareth Stevens
PUBLISHING

Please visit our website, www.garethstevens.com. For a free color catalog of all our high-quality books, call toll free 1-800-542-2595 or fax 1-877-542-2596.

Cataloging-in-Publication Data

Names: Hibbert, Clare. | Farkas, Rudolf.
Title: Vertebrates / by Clare Hibbert and Rudolf Farkas.
Description: New York : Gareth Stevens Publishing, 2023. | Series: Prehistoric life | Includes glossary and index.
Identifiers: ISBN 9781538284612 (pbk.) | ISBN 9781538284629 (library bound) | ISBN 9781538284636 (ebook)
Subjects: LCSH: Animals, Fossil--Juvenile literature. | Mammals, Fossil--Juvenile literature.
Classification: LCC QE881.H53 2023 | DDC 569--dc23

Published in 2023 by
Gareth Stevens Publishing
2544 Clinton St.
Buffalo, NY 14224

Series Editor: Amy Pimperton
Series Designer: Peter Scoulding
Picture Researcher: Diana Morris

Picture Credits
Beatrissa/Shutterstock: 6.
Houston Museum of Natural Science, Houston, Texas. Daderot/CC Wikimedia Commons: 4.
Maija Karala/CC Wikimedia Commons: 5.
Mopic/Shutterstock: 7.

Printed in the United States of America

CPSIA compliance information: Batch #CWGS23: For further information contact Gareth Stevens at 1-800-542-2595.

Find us on

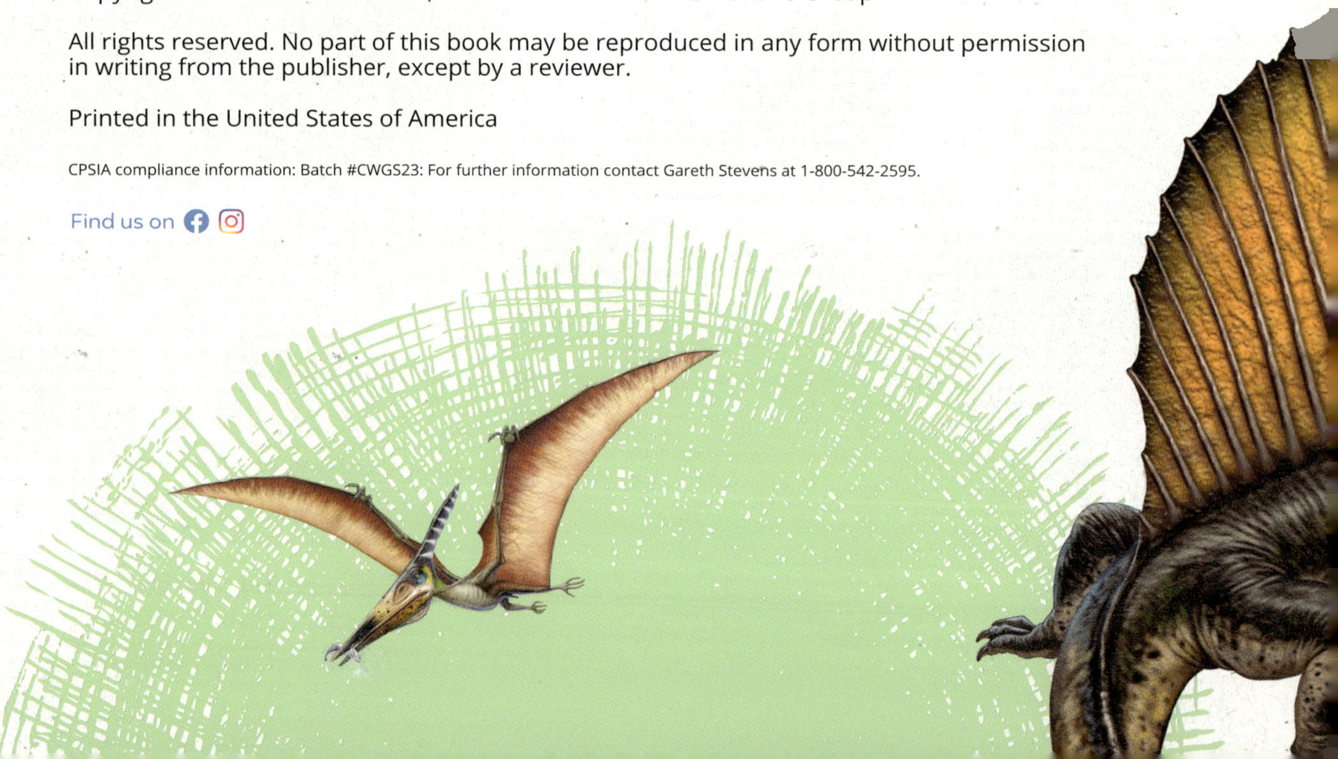

CONTENTS

THE FIRST ANIMALS

Dinosaurs are the best-known prehistoric beasts. However, countless other animal groups appeared—and died out—in the billions of years before humans appeared on Earth.

FOSSIL EVIDENCE

Fossils are the preserved remains of animals that, over millions of years, have been turned into rock. Each new fossil discovery tells us more about the animals of the past.

The study of fossils is called palaeontology. This fossilized skeleton is an Archegosaurus, *a salamander-like animal that lived 299–253 million years ago (mya).*

From sea to land

Animals are organisms made up of many cells and are able to move, eat, and reproduce. The first animals were invertebrates, or animals without backbones. Even today, around 97 percent of all animal species on Earth are invertebrates. They include insects, spiders, crabs, snails, and starfish. This book is about vertebrate animals, or those with backbones. Only 3 percent of animal species are vertebrates.

Fish, the first vertebrates, appeared in the ocean around 500 mya.* About 100 million years later, four-legged fish crawled out of the ocean and onto land. They were the ancestors of all land vertebrates, including birds and mammals.

*All the dates in this book are approximate.

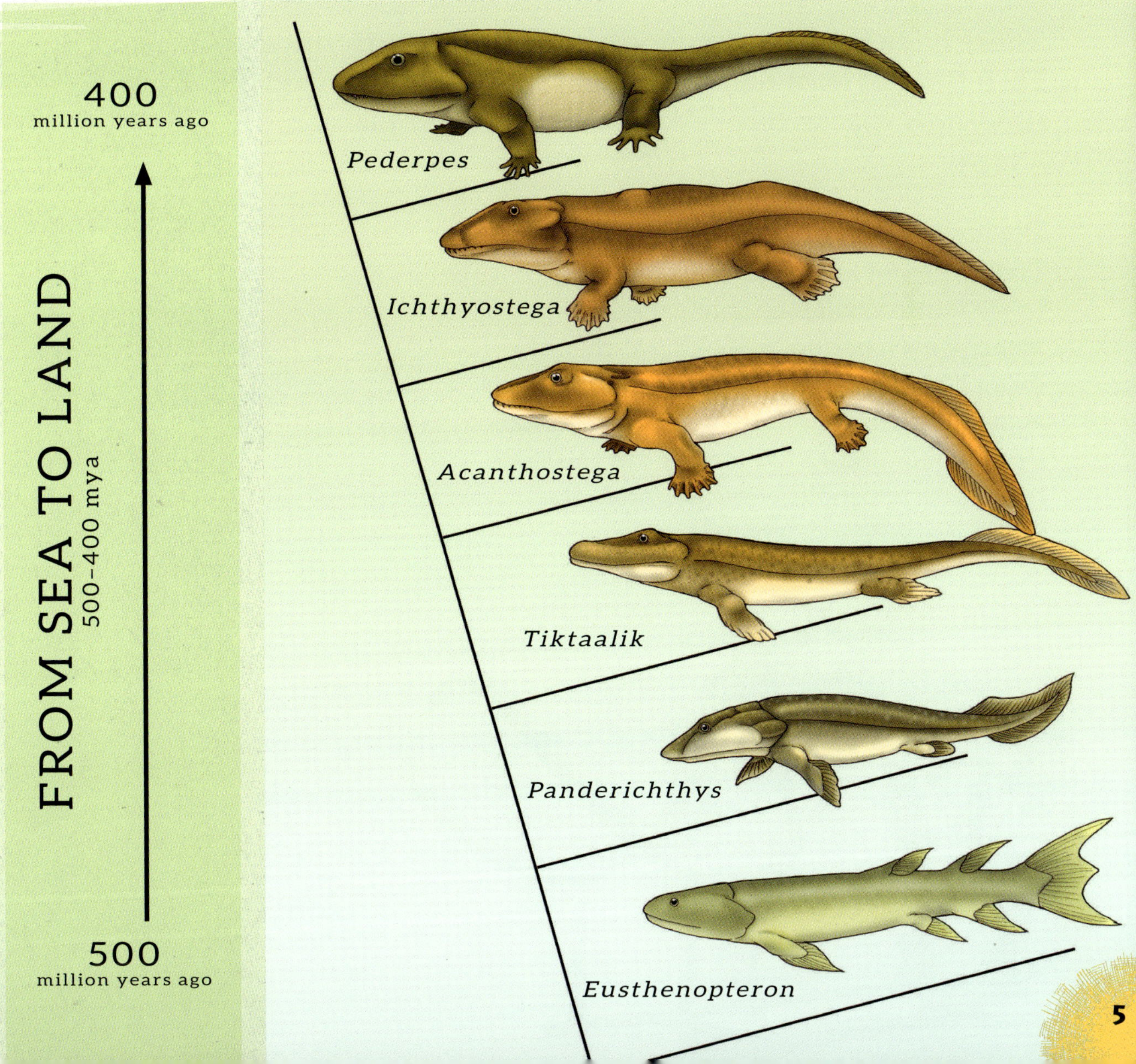

ENDINGS AND BEGINNINGS

There have been five major extinctions on Earth since life began. Each time, at least half the animal species were wiped out. Each time, new species have evolved to take their place.

Periods of time

The history of life on Earth is mind-boggling. Geologists break it into smaller chunks called periods. They identify each period by looking at the rocks that formed at that time. The first mammal fossils appear in rocks from the Cretaceous Period. Woolly mammoths, which lived at the same time as early people, were around in the Quaternary Period, which is still going on.

MYTHS AND STORIES

Before modern science, fossilized jaws and other bones must have been puzzling and even frightening. Perhaps they inspired people to make up stories about monsters, dragons and other mythical beasts.

Complete skeletons of prehistoric animals are very rare. This mammoth skeleton is about 80 percent fossilized bone. The remaining 20 percent is made of resin.

Animals appeared in the Cambrian Period. The big stretch of time from when Earth formed until the start of the Cambrian Period is called the Precambrian Eon, which occurred 4,600–541 mya.

Period	Million years ago	Major extinction event
Cambrian	541–485	
Ordovician	485–443	
		First: 455–430 mya
Silurian	443–419	
Devonian	419–359	
		Second: 407–359 mya
Carboniferous	359–299	
		Third: 266–252 mya
Permian	299–252	
Triassic	252–201	
		Fourth: 201 mya
Jurassic	201–145	
Cretaceous	145–66	
		Fifth: 66 mya
Palaeogene	66–23	
Neogene	23–2.6	
Quaternary	2.6–Today	

An asteroid hitting Earth probably caused the big extinction at the end of the Cretaceous Period. It threw up enough dust to block out sunlight for decades.

DIMETRODON

PRONUNCIATION:	*die-MEET-ruh-don*
GROUP:	Synapsids
LIVED:	Permian Period, 295–272 mya
RANGE:	Europe, North America
HABITAT:	Dry scrubland, wetland
WEIGHT:	550 pounds (250 kg)
LENGTH:	11 feet (3.5 m)

The fearsome predator *Dimetrodon* lived more than 40 million years before the first dinosaurs and was bigger than a family car. It ate fish, amphibians, and reptiles.

Dimetrodon had an enormous sail on its back, which was supported by rods that branched out from its spine. The sail gave the animal's body more surface area, so it could heat up quickly in the morning when it basked in the sun. Like today's reptiles, *Dimetrodon* was not able to make its own body heat. *Dimetrodon* might have also used its sail to threaten attackers or impress a mate.

TOOTH TYPES

Dimetrodon was a carnivore, and its short snout was packed with more than 80 teeth—sharp canines at the front and broader teeth at the back for grinding up muscle and bone. The name *Dimetrodon* means "two measures of teeth."

Dimetrodon's *legs splayed out to the side like a lizard's—they weren't upright like a dinosaur's.*

TEMNODONTOSAURUS

PRONUNCIATION:	*tem-no-DONT-uh-SAWR-us*
CLASS:	Reptiles
LIVED:	Early Jurassic Period, 200–175 mya
RANGE:	Europe
HABITAT:	Deep or open ocean
WEIGHT:	5 tons (4.5 tonnes)
LENGTH:	39 feet (12 m)

***Temnodontosaurus* was a gigantic ichthyosaur—one of the dolphin-shaped marine reptiles that lived in dinosaur times. In spite of their fishy appearance, ichthyosaurs could not breathe underwater and had to come up to the surface for air.**

LIVE BABIES

Most reptile babies hatch from eggs, but ichthyosaur mothers developed the eggs inside their bodies and then gave birth to live young. This is called being viviparous, and some snakes reproduce like that today.

Most ichthyosaurs were about 9.8 feet (3 m) long, but *Temnodontosaurus* was four times that! Its most striking feature was its dinner-plate-sized eyes, which were probably the largest eyes of any animal on Earth, ever. At 8 inches (20 cm) across, they helped it to see in its gloomy, deep-ocean home. This predator slipped through Jurassic seas looking for squid, fish, plesiosaurs, and other prey.

Temnodontosaurus *even hunted other ichthyosaurs, such as the much smaller* Stenopterygius.

>

PTERANODON

PRONUNCIATION:	*ter-AN-oh-don*
CLASS:	Reptiles
LIVED:	Late Cretaceous Period, 86–84.5 mya
RANGE:	North America
HABITAT:	Coastal areas
WEIGHT:	55 pounds (25 kg)
LENGTH:	6 feet (1.8 m)

***Pteranodon* was a large pterosaur, one of the flying reptiles that swooped through the skies 215 to 66 mya. Over 1,200 *Pteranodon* fossils have been found—more than of any other pterosaur.**

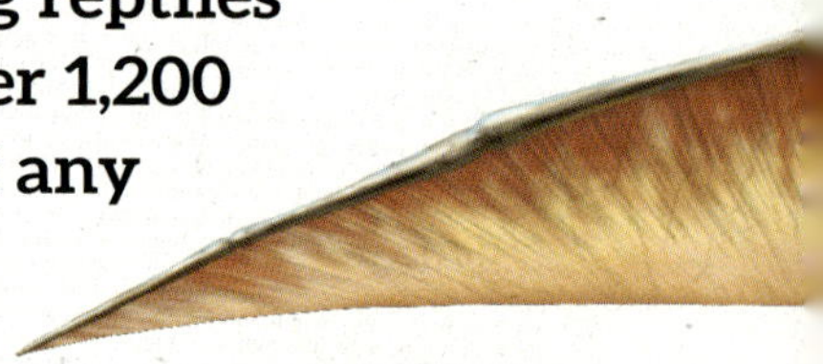

BIRD-LIKE BEAK

Pteranodon's name means "wing without tooth." Unlike earlier pterosaurs, it did not have any teeth. Its jaw was more like a bird's beak. *Pteranodon* must have gulped down fish whole, just like a pelican!

With a wingspan of 20 feet (6 m), *Pteranodon* was larger than any of today's seabirds, but it probably fed in a similar way. It could have flown low over the sea and snatched fish swimming near the surface. It was also the perfect, streamlined shape for diving headfirst into the water like a gannet, thanks to its long, sharp beak and backwards-pointing head crest. *Pteranodon* probably showed off its crest to attract a mate.

Pteranodon's *large wings made it an expert at gliding, but it could also flap its wings. Before the pterosaurs, only insects had managed to fly.* >

ELASMOSAURUS

PRONUNCIATION:	*ee-LAZ-moh-SAWR-us*
CLASS:	Reptiles
LIVED:	Late Cretaceous Period, 80.5 mya
RANGE:	North America
HABITAT:	Open ocean
WEIGHT:	2.2 tons (2 tonnes)
LENGTH:	38 feet (10.3 m)

Plesiosaurs were long-necked marine reptiles that lived at the same time as dinosaurs and pterosaurs. One group had particularly long necks. They are called elasmosaurs, and were named after *Elasmosaurus*, which was the first one to be discovered.

Like many marine hunters, *Elasmosaurus* probably had a dark back and a light belly. Its coloring would have helped it blend in with the seabed when viewed from above, and with the glimmering surface of the sea when viewed from underneath. A slow swimmer, it probably approached shoals of fish from below, then bobbed up its head to gulp down as many as it could before they all swam off.

PAIN IN THE NECK?

Elasmosaurus's long neck took up more than half its body length! It contained more than 70 neck bones. By comparison, a giraffe has only seven. No land animal could ever support a neck as long as *Elasmosaurus*'s.

Elasmosaurus *gulped down its catch without chewing. Stones in its gut helped to grind up its food.*

MOSASAURUS

PRONUNCIATION:	*MOZ-uh-SAWR-us*
CLASS:	Reptiles
LIVED:	Late Cretaceous Period, 70–66 mya
RANGE:	Western Europe and North America
HABITAT:	Oceans and shallow seas
WEIGHT:	5.5 tons (5 tonnes)
HEIGHT:	47.5 feet (14.5 m)

Mosasaurs are a group of reptiles that take their name from *Mosasaurus*, a ferocious marine predator that lived at the end of the Cretaceous Period. Mosasaurs hunted the same foods as ichthyosaurs and were so successful that their rivals became extinct!

Mosasaurus had a large head and a sleek but massive body. It hunted turtles, plesiosaurs, ichthyosaurs, and smaller mosasaurs. Like modern snakes, it had a double-hinged jaw that allowed it to swallow prey whole. *Mosasaurus* waved its tail up and down to cruise through the water and steered with its flippers. This reptile could not support its body on land. Instead, it gave birth to live young in the water.

CUVIER'S CLUE

The first *Mosasaurus* fossil, a skull, was found just outside Maastricht (now in the Netherlands) in 1764. French scientist Georges Cuvier (1769-1832) mentioned the find as proof in his theory about cycles of extinction in the animal kingdom.

Mosasaurus's *long, narrow jaw contained 40 to 50 sharp, cone-shaped teeth.*

MEGALODON

PRONUNCIATION:	*MEG-a-LOH-don*
CLASS:	Cartilaginous fish
LIVED:	Neogene Period, 16–2.6 mya
RANGE:	Warm, coastal waters
HABITAT:	Worldwide
WEIGHT:	80 tons (73 tonnes)
LENGTH:	60 feet (18 m)

Monstrous megalodon was one of the largest hunters to ever live on Earth. This outsize shark was three times the length of today's great white shark.

THE STORY OF SHARKS

Sharks first appeared around 450 mya—long before the dinosaurs. They are one of our planet's oldest life forms. Today, there are more than 500 shark species swimming in the oceans.

Sharks belong to a group of fish that have skeletons made of cartilage instead of bone. Cartilage does not fossilize as easily as bone, so prehistoric sharks are known only from their teeth. Their body sizes are based on guesswork! Megalodon's teeth were more than 6 inches (15 cm) long. Its jaws had a bite force of up to 41,000 pounds (18,600 kg) —strong enough to crush a whale's skull.

Megalodon consumed about a ton of food every day! It hunted marine mammals, such as whales, dolphins, and porpoises.

PHORUSRHACOS

PRONUNCIATION:	*FOE-roos-RAY-cuss*
CLASS:	Birds
LIVED:	Early Neogene Period, 12 mya
RANGE:	South America
HABITAT:	Grassland
WEIGHT:	300 pounds (136 kg)
HEIGHT:	8 feet (2.4 m)

Better known as the "terror bird," *Phorusrhacos* was truly terrifying. It was slightly shorter than an ostrich, with a huge head and a massive, hooked beak for tearing into flesh.

Too heavy to fly, *Phorusrhacos* was able to hit speeds of 30 miles (48 km) per hour thanks to its long, muscular legs—although it was not as fast as an ostrich. Once it had chased down its mammal prey, the terror bird gripped it in its talons and chowed down with its beak. It might have thrown larger prey against a rock in order to stun it and break its bones.

DINOSAUR DESCENDANTS

All birds, including the terror bird, evolved from dinosaurs. They survived the great extinction of 66 million years ago that wiped out other dinosaurs, pterosaurs, and plesiosaurs.

Almost two-thirds of the terror bird's huge skull was made up of its deadly, curved beak. >

MEGATHERIUM

PRONUNCIATION:	*MEG-a-theer-EE-um*
CLASS:	Mammals
LIVED:	Neogene Period to Quaternary Period, 5 mya – 11,000 years ago (ya)
RANGE:	South America
HABITAT:	Woodland, grassland
WEIGHT:	4.4 tons (4 tonnes)
LENGTH:	20 feet (6 m)

Elephant-sized *Megatherium* was one of the largest land mammals ever. Also known as the giant ground sloth, its closest living relatives are anteaters, armadillos, and tree sloths.

Megatherium was one of the enormous animals that evolved to fill the gap that was left behind when the dinosaurs died out. Others included giant beavers, wombats, deer, horses, and rhinos. Like these, *Megatherium* was a herbivore. It could rear up to rip branches off trees with its massive, clawed "hands." Under its shaggy coat, bony plates called osteoderms helped to keep in body heat and protect it from predators.

THE END

Megatherium became extinct around the end of the Ice Age, about 11,000 years ago. It probably could not cope with the warmer climate. It is also possible that this slow-moving giant was an easy target for human hunter-gatherers.

Megatherium *moved around on all-fours, but sometimes reared up to feed. Its tail helped it to balance.* >

SMILODON

PRONUNCIATION:	*SMILE-oh-don*
CLASS:	Mammals
LIVED:	Quaternary Period, 2.5 mya – 10,000 ya
RANGE:	North and South America
HABITAT:	Woodland, grassland
WEIGHT:	880 pounds (400 kg)
LENGTH:	7.4 feet (2.25 m)

Smilodon was the biggest feline ever, as heavy as four jaguars! Its nickname, the saber-toothed tiger, comes from its canine teeth—curved fangs that were up to 12 inches (30 cm) long.

Smilodon was an apex predator. It hunted deer, buffalo, camels, ground sloths, and even mammoths. Its hunting technique was to lie in wait in the low branches of a tree. When prey passed below, it leapt down and ambushed it, delivering a killer bite. *Smilodon* could open its jaws twice as wide as a lion can, but if it broke either of its canine teeth, they never grew back.

PACK LIFE?

Some *Smilodon* fossils show signs of wounds that had time to heal. A solitary hunter with serious injuries would have died of starvation. It is possible that *Smilodon* lived in packs, like modern lions.

Smilodon*'s outsize fangs could stab and slash at prey, such as these bison.*

WOOLLY MAMMOTH

CLASS: Mammals
LIVED: Quaternary Period, 400,000–10,000 ya
RANGE: Eurasia, North America
HABITAT: Grasslands
WEIGHT: up to 6.6 tons (6 tonnes)
HEIGHT: 11.5 feet (3.5 m) (at shoulder)

Mammoths were huge, hairy members of the elephant family. They lived on the grasslands of Europe, Asia, and the Americas until just after the last Ice Age.

Unlike modern elephants, which have evolved large, flappable ears to stay cool, mammoths had small ears that didn't lose body heat. Other adaptations for life in a cold climate included a thick, shaggy coat and big, bulky body. The fatty hump behind the mammoth's head stored energy, just like a camel's hump, so the animal could survive in the coldest months when food was scarce.

TERRIFIC TUSKS

Mammoths' long, curved tusks kept growing throughout their life. They were a good defense against attackers, such as saber-toothed tigers. They could also be used to clear away snow to get at plants underneath.

Mammoths lived in family groups called herds, just like elephants today. >

TIMELINE

This timeline shows the different periods, or chunks of time, since life began on Earth. It includes the appearance of key species in this book, as well as when some of them became extinct.*

Eon

Precambrian 4,600–541 mya

3,600 mya	First life forms as bacteria.
640 mya	First animals (sponges) appear.

Era Period

PALAEOZOIC 541–252 mya

Cambrian 541–485 mya

Ordovician 485–443 mya

455–430 mya	The first major extinction wipes out 85 percent of all species.

Silurian 443–419 mya

Devonian 419–359 mya

400 mya	Ammonites, flying insects, and first land vertebrates appear.
407–359 mya	The second major extinction wipes out 75 percent of animal species, including all land vertebrates.

Carboniferous 359–299 mya

354 mya	Land vertebrates evolve again.

Permian 299–252 mya

295–272 mya	*Dimetrodon*
266–252 mya	A third major extinction wipes out 95 percent of marine species and 70 percent of land species.

* All the dates on these pages are approximate.

Era	Period		
MESOZOIC 252–66 mya	**Triassic 252–201 mya**		
		250–215 mya	Dinosaurs, pterosaurs, and plesiosaurs appear.
		201 mya	The fourth major extinction wipes out 76 percent of all species.
	Jurassic 201–145 mya		
		200–175 mya	*Temnodontosaurus*
	Cretaceous 145–66 mya		
		86–84.5 mya	*Pteranodon*
		80.5 mya	*Elasmosaurus*
		70–66 mya	*Mosasaurus*
		66 mya	A fifth major extinction wipes out 80 percent of animal species, including non-avian dinosaurs, pterosaurs, plesiosaurs, and more.
CENOZOIC 66 mya–TODAY	**Palaeogene 66–23 mya**		
	Neogene 23–2.6 mya		
		16–2.6 mya	Megalodon
		12 mya	*Phorusrhacos*
		5 mya – 11,000 ya	*Megatherium*
	Quaternary 2.6 mya – today		
		2.5 mya – 10,000 ya	*Smilodon*
		400,000–10,000 ya	Woolly mammoth
		200,000 ya	Our species, *Homo sapiens*, appears in Africa.

GLOSSARY

amphibian An animal with a bony skeleton and slimy skin that lives partly on land, partly in water, and cannot make its own body heat
canine tooth A long, sharp tooth found near the front of the mouth in carnivores
carnivore A meat-eater
cartilage Tough, flexible tissue attached to a bone, such as the tip of a human nose
cell The smallest part of a living thing that is able to function independently
climate The average weather of a place over a long period of time
dinosaur An extinct land reptile from the Triassic, Jurassic, or Cretaceous periods whose legs came straight down from its body rather than splaying out like a modern reptile's
evolve To change over millions of years, by passing on useful characteristics through the generations
extinct An animal or plant that has died out
fossil The remains of an animal or plant that died long ago, preserved in rock
habitat The natural home of a plant or animal
herbivore A plant-eater
hunter-gatherer Someone who lives by hunting, fishing, and collecting wild foods
Ice Age The last time that the climate was so cold that huge ice sheets covered much of Earth, around 21,000 to 11,500 years ago.
ichthyosaur A dolphin-like, predatory marine reptile that lived in the Triassic, Jurassic, and Cretaceous periods
invertebrate An animal without a backbone. Insects, spiders, worms, crabs, and jellyfish are all invertebrates.
mammal An animal with a bony skeleton and fur or hair, and that can make its own body heat and feeds its babies milk
marine Of or from the ocean
organism A single living thing, such as a plant or an animal
osteoderm The bony scales or plates usually found on a reptile's skin
palaeontology The branch of science concerned with the study of fossils
plesiosaur A long-necked, predatory marine reptile that lived in the Jurassic and Cretaceous periods
predator An animal that hunts other animals for food
prehistoric From the time before written records
prey An animal that is hunted by other animals for food
pterosaur A flying reptile with wings made from skin stretched over a long fourth finger
reptile An animal with a bony skeleton and scaly skin that cannot make its own body heat
resin A human-made material that is often used in making some plastics
saber-toothed Describes an animal with long, curved canine teeth
salamander A small amphibian with a long, slender body and tail, and four short legs. Its skin often has brightly colored markings.
species One particular type of living thing. Members of the same species look like each other and can reproduce together.
synapsid A primitive mammal
vertebrate An animal with a backbone. Fish, amphibians, reptiles, and mammals (including humans) are all vertebrates.
viviparous Producing live young that developed inside the parent's body instead of laying eggs

FURTHER INFORMATION

Books:

Gagne, Tammy. *Megalodon and Other Prehistoric Sharks.* North Mankato, MN: Capstone Press, 2022.

Hansen, Grace. *Dinosaur Graveyards in North America.* Minneapolis, MN: Abdo Kids Jumbo, an imprint of Abdo Kids, 2022.

Taylor, Barbara. *The Magnificent Book of Extinct Animals.* San Rafael, CA: Weldon Owen Children's Books, 2022.

Websites:

kids.nationalgeographic.com/animals/prehistoric/facts/woolly-mammoth
Check out the National Geographic Kids guide to the woolly mammoth.

www.natgeokids.com/uk/category/discover/animals/prehistoric-animals/
Read about prehistoric animals here.

Places:

Caspersen Beach, Venice, Florida

Fossil Butte National Monument, Kemmerer, Wyoming

The Mammoth Site, Hot Springs, Colorado

La Brea Tar Pits, Los Angeles, California

Publisher's note to educators and parents: Our editors have carefully reviewed these websites to ensure that they are suitable for students. Many websites change frequently, however, and we cannot guarantee that a site's future contents will continue to meet our high standards of quality and educational value. Be advised that students should be closely supervised whenever they access the internet.

INDEX